Mysteries in Space

A CHAPTER BOOK

Rosanna Hansen

children's press®

A Division of Scholastic Inc.
New York Toronto London Auckland Sydney
Mexico City New Delhi Hong Kong
Danbury, Connecticut

To CRH, the brightest star in my galaxy

ACKNOWLEDGMENTS

The author and publisher would like to thank all those who gave their time
and knowledge to help with this book. In particular, special thanks go to
Dr. James Oberg; Dr. Jon D. Pelletier, Department of Geosciences, University
of Arizona; and Dr. David H. Hathaway, NASA/Marshall Space Flight Center.

Library of Congress Cataloging-in-Publication Data

Hansen, Rosanna.
  Mysteries in space : a chapter book / by Rosanna Hansen.
      p. cm. — (True tales)
  Includes bibliographical references and index.
  ISBN 0-516-25185-6 (lib. bdg.)   0-516-25450-2 (pbk.)
  1. Astronomy—Miscellanea—Juvenile literature. I. Title. II.
Series.
  QB46.H185 2005
  523—dc22
                              2005005521

1 2 3 4 5 6 7 8 9 10 R 14 13 12 11 10 09 08 07 06 05

CONTENTS

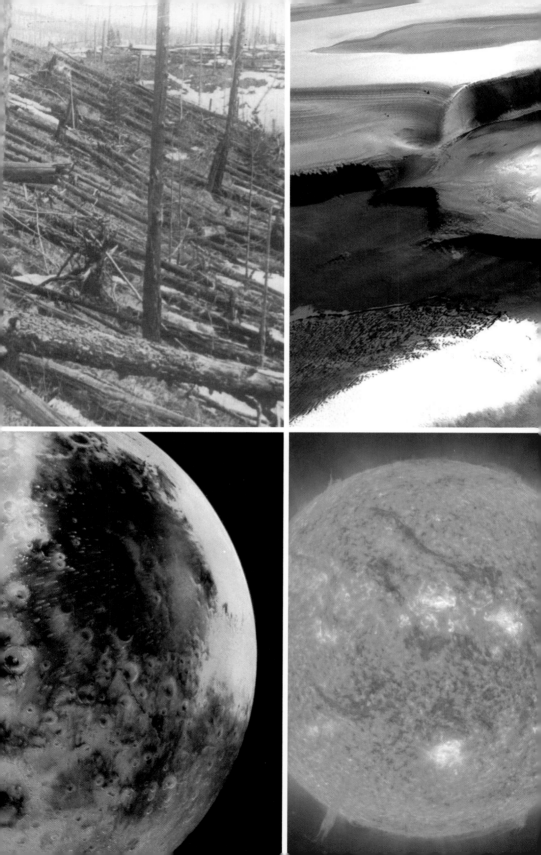

INTRODUCTION

Our sun and the planets that circle it are full of mysteries. People have wondered about these mysteries for many years.

Why do objects like **asteroids** and **comets** sometimes zoom toward Earth, coming so close that they make terrible explosions? When a huge fireball exploded in 1908, was it an asteroid—or an alien spaceship?

Why does Mars have strange spirals in its polar ice caps? And could there be life on the planet?

Why does the sun have strange spots on its surface? Why do these **sunspots** build up to a stormy peak every eleven years? Most importantly, why do the sunspots and even bigger sun storms cause trouble for people here on Earth?

These and other mysteries keep space scientists busy looking for answers. Here are the true stories of four space mysteries and the scientists who are working to solve them.

CHAPTER ONE

A MYSTERIOUS FIREBALL

One morning in 1908, people in Siberia, Russia, saw a huge fireball soar in from space. As they stared, the fireball zoomed close to Earth. Suddenly, the fireball exploded with a terrifying blast.

In the forest below, herds of reindeer fell down and died. Trees fell and burned within a circle more than 25 miles (40 kilometers) wide. People in a town 50 miles (81 kilometers) away felt the earth shake violently. As it shook, they

This photograph, taken almost twenty years after the explosion, shows the damage done to the area.

saw their homes sway and windows shatter into bits. People screamed and wept as a mushroom-shaped cloud rose in the sky.

In London, almost 4,000 miles (6,437 kilometers) from Siberia, the huge blast showed up on earthquake monitors. For several nights afterward, the sky over all of Europe glowed like daylight. At midnight, it was light enough for people in Paris and London to go outside and read.

Today, the fireball explosion is still a mystery. We call it the Tunguska fireball because it flew toward Earth near the Stony Tunguska River in the Siberian wilderness.

This is a photograph of a hydrogen-bomb explosion. The explosion in Tunguska was as powerful as ten of these bombs.

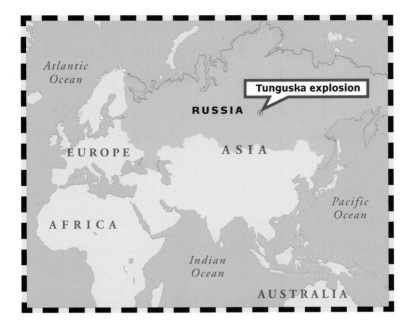

Atlantic Ocean

RUSSIA

Tunguska explosion

EUROPE

ASIA

Pacific Ocean

AFRICA

Indian Ocean

AUSTRALIA

Scientists now know the Tunguska explosion was as powerful as the force of ten **hydrogen bombs**. That means the Tunguska blast was the most powerful explosion in recorded history.

The Tunguska River is in a **remote** part of Siberia. This bitterly cold land is full of swamps and thick forests. Only a few people live nearby. So scientists didn't visit the site of the explosion until almost twenty years afterward. It was just too hard to reach Tunguska.

In 1927, scientists finally traveled to the site of the Tunguska blast for the first time.

They were amazed by what they found. The immense explosion had left no crater, or hole. All the scientists could find was broken and burned trees that had fallen in a huge butterfly pattern starting from the middle of the site. The scientists had hoped to find some pieces of metal or stone left by whatever was inside the fireball, but they found neither.

Since 1908, many newspapers and magazines have published articles about the mysterious fireball. Some writers said they thought the fireball was really a spaceship

Some people wondered if the fireball was an alien spaceship, like the model in this photograph.

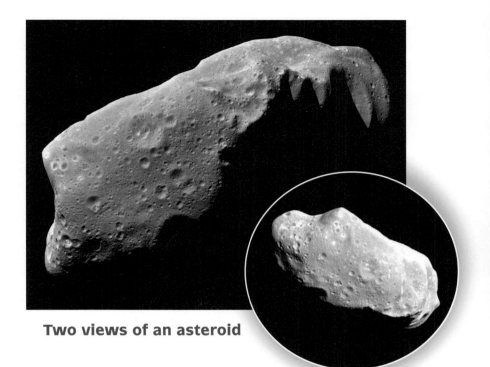

Two views of an asteroid

carrying aliens. The writers even said that
perhaps the spaceship had exploded before
landing. Scientists studying the blast have
recently come up with more realistic
theories. Most scientists today think that
the fireball was either an asteroid or a comet.

Asteroids are large chunks of rock that
float in space. Most asteroids circle the sun
in a band called the asteroid belt. Sometimes
an asteroid spins out of **orbit**, flying off
through the **solar system**. A few of these
asteroids head toward Earth.

If the fireball was an asteroid, why hasn't a crater, like the one above, been found?

Some scientists believe the Tunguska fireball began as a huge asteroid. Their theory is that the asteroid flew through space and entered Earth's **atmosphere** at nearly 50,000 miles (80,465 kilometers) per hour. As it flew, it rubbed against the atmosphere, grew red-hot, and burst into flames. The huge fireball plunged down and blew apart about 6 miles (about 10 kilometers) above Tunguska.

Questions remain about the asteroid theory. If the Tunguska fireball was an asteroid, why aren't there any pieces left? And why isn't there any crater near the explosion? In response, some scientists say that part of the asteroid may have been ground into dust when it exploded. Another part of the asteroid could have been blown in a different direction, zooming off into space again. In that case, no pieces of the asteroid would be left.

Other scientists think the strange fireball began as a comet. Out in space, comets are big, dirty snowballs. They have an icy center covered with black dust.

A bright comet zooms through space.

When comets fly close to the sun, their icy cores become gas. They start to glow, and their gases stream out into long tails. Once in a while, a comet flies quite close to Earth. Some scientists think that a large comet flew too close to Earth and exploded at Tunguska.

The asteroid and comet theories both look promising, but neither has been proven. More scientific work must be done. Only then will the mystery be completely solved.

Tunguska as it looks today

CHAPTER TWO

THE MYSTERY OF THE SPIRAL CANYONS

People have wondered about the mysterious planet Mars for hundreds of years. After all, Mars is one of our nearest neighbors in space. It's the next planet after Earth in our solar system. Also, Mars has many unsolved mysteries. One of the most intriguing mysteries was found at Mars' North and South **poles**.

Mars and Earth are alike in some ways. For one thing, Earth has ice caps at its North and South poles. So does Mars.

Earth

Like Earth, Mars has ice caps at its northern
and southern poles.

The Hubble Space Telescope

Scientists were surprised to find ice caps or water in any form on Mars, because most of Mars is bone dry. Except for its polar ice caps, Mars is covered with reddish dirt and rock. In fact, its nickname is the Red Planet.

The **Hubble Space Telescope** took pictures of Mars' northern ice cap. The pictures show how the ice cap changes during the Martian year. The northern ice cap is mostly frozen water, topped by some frozen **carbon dioxide**. The ice increases as the temperature drops in the fall and winter. Then, as the weather warms up in spring, the ice cap shrinks.

For years, scientists have studied both the northern and southern ice caps on Mars. The scientists found that the ice caps have beautiful, icy canyons. These canyons spiral down as deep as 3,000 feet (914 meters)! The huge canyons curve out like the arms of a pinwheel. Their swirls look like the spirals of a giant seashell or the spinning arms of a hurricane.

The northern ice cap on Mars

Jon Pelletier

Scientists could not figure out why the canyons had such odd, pinwheel shapes. In 2003, a scientist named Jon Pelletier had an idea about the canyons. He based this idea on his research and on special computer models.

Jon pointed out that Mars tilts to one side as it circles, or orbits, the sun. This tilt means that the sun hits the icy walls of the canyon unevenly. The sun warms the ice,

Mars tilts as it goes around the sun.

which starts to melt. Then, the melting ice changes into water vapor, or gas. As the ice melts, the sunny side of the canyon gets wider and deeper.

Next, the water vapor hits the dark, cold side of the canyon. The water vapor condenses and refreezes into ice. The new ice makes the dark side of the canyon get bigger. As this process happens over and over, the icy canyons spiral down, getting deeper each year.

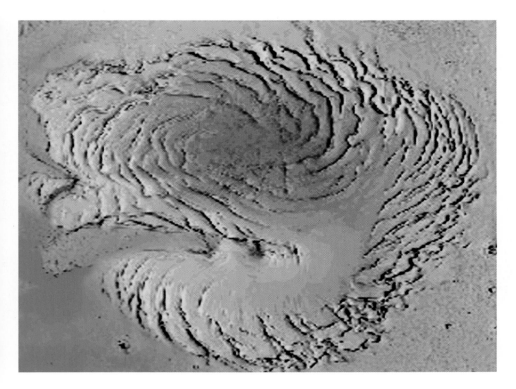

The canyons on Mars look like the arms of a pinwheel.

Jon's computer model shows how the canyons on Mars were formed.

Today, the canyons spiral down more than half a mile (804 meters). Their icy spirals now cover hundreds of miles of polar ice. They form the biggest, iciest pinwheel ever!

Jon Pelletier thinks that the melting and refreezing of the canyons is the reason for their spiral shape. To prove his theory, Jon has created computer images, using the information many scientists have gathered about the canyons. Jon's computer images are an exact match for the icy spirals, right down to a few little nicks and cracks.

"The computer model shows how the canyons are curved, and how they evolve over time to create spirals," says Jon. Thanks to his work, we now have an explanation for these mysterious Martian spirals.

**The northern ice cap on Mars can be seen
at the top of this photograph.**

CHAPTER THREE

LIFE ON MARS?

Is there life on Mars? This question has interested scientists ever since the planet was discovered. Then, about a hundred years ago, an Italian astronomer named Giovanni Schiaparelli said he had seen *canali*, or channels, on Mars.

Some people thought the word *canali* meant canals. They began to imagine creatures living on Mars, digging canals and building homes. Soon, books and movies about strange creatures from Mars became popular. They have been popular ever since.

Giovanni Schiaparelli

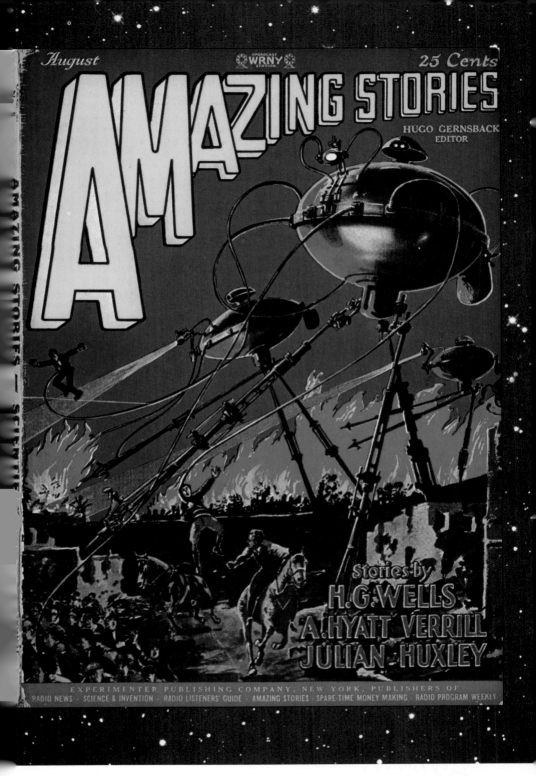

The cover of this 1926 science-fiction magazine shows
Martians invading Earth.

In some important ways, Mars is like Earth. Mars has seasons, weather, dirt, rocks, mountains, and polar caps—just like Earth.

In many other ways, though, Mars is very different from Earth. Mars is a reddish, dusty world. It is much colder and drier than Earth. No green plants grow on Mars, and no water flows on its surface. As far as we can tell, no plants or other life forms exist on the surface of Mars today.

Scientists say that Mars was once a very different place. About four billion years ago, Mars may have been much warmer. Back then, Mars probably had water on its surface. Most exciting of all, Mars may once have had tiny forms of life somewhere in its soil.

In the 1970s, scientists began sending unmanned spacecraft to Mars, hoping to find life there. They tested several samples

Martian landscape

of Martian soil. Although the Martian dirt did not show any signs of life, the scientists did not give up hope.

Then, in 1996, NASA scientists made an exciting discovery. They were studying a **meteorite** that had fallen to Earth from Mars. In this meteorite, the scientists found tiny gold-colored specks. The tiny specks contain chemicals. The NASA scientists say these chemicals may have come from tiny living things that once existed on Mars.

This meteorite once was part of Mars.
It fell to Earth 13,000 years ago.

This *Pathfinder* robot gathered soil and rocks on Mars.

A year later, in 1997, a *Pathfinder* robot found rocks from **volcanoes** on Mars. These volcanic rocks were another sign that life could once have existed on Mars long ago.

About four billion years ago, hot melted rocks called lava flowed out of Mars' volcanoes and slowly hardened. At the time, the exploding volcanoes and hot lava may have provided the spark of energy needed for life to begin on Mars.

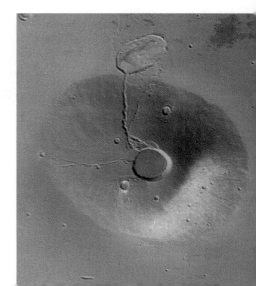

Martian volcano

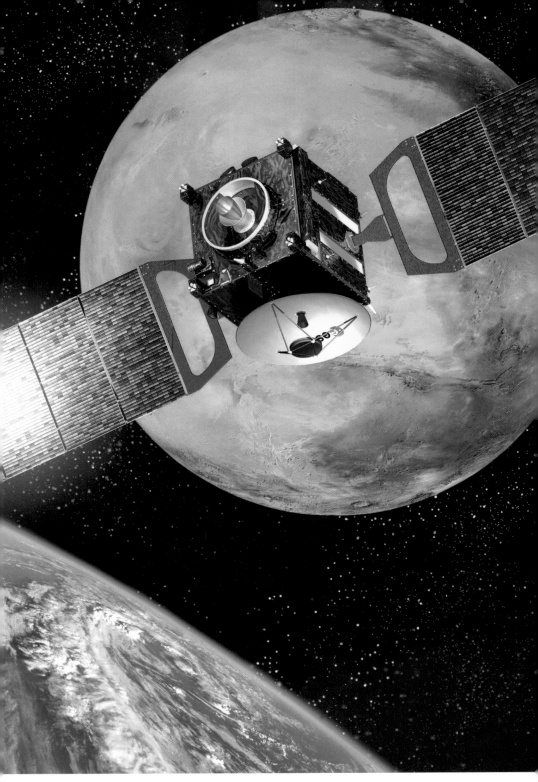

The *Mars Express* spacecraft helped scientists find
out that methane exists on Mars.

In 2004, NASA scientists made another exciting discovery. They found that the atmosphere on Mars contains a chemical called **methane**. Some kinds of bacteria breathe out methane as a waste product. Bacteria are tiny living creatures too small to see except through a microscope. The fact that there is methane on Mars may mean that bacteria are alive somewhere on Mars.

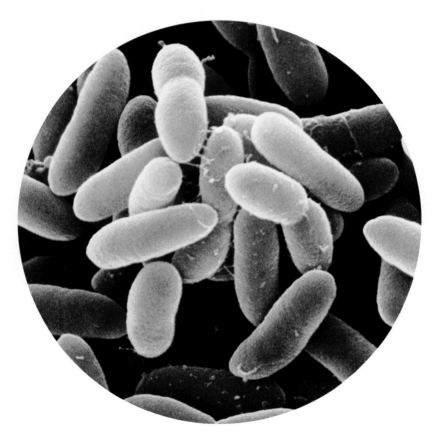

Bacteria are one of the smallest life forms on Earth. Do they exist on Mars, too?

If these bacteria do exist, where would they live? Scientists say the bacteria would probably live beneath the surface of Mars. That's why no bacteria have been found in the soil samples taken from Mars' surface.

So, is there life on Mars? No one knows for sure yet. Many scientists think that the recent discoveries are very promising. They hope that someday soon we will have definite proof of life on Mars.

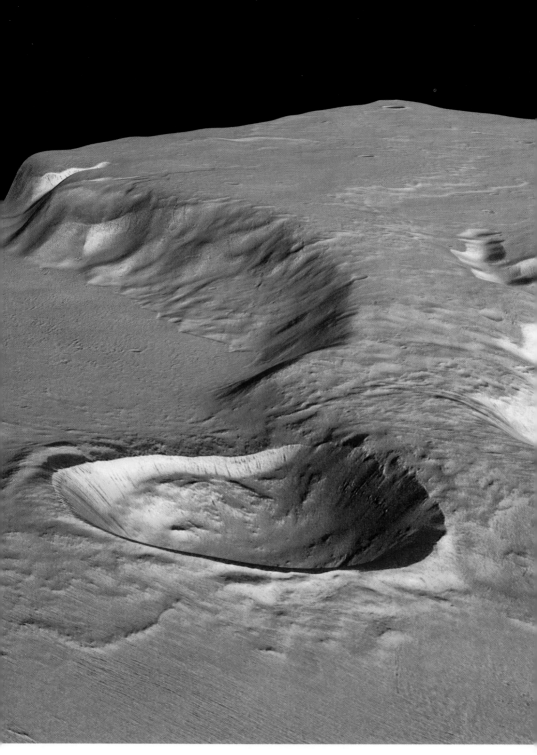

Will life be found on Mars one day?

CHAPTER FOUR

THE SUN'S MYSTERIOUS SPOTS

Did you know our sun has strange spots on its surface? These **sunspots** look a little bit like dark freckles. Scientists now know that sunspots are really magnetic storms that break out on the sun. The scientists also know that the number of sunspots and other storms on the sun builds up to a peak every eleven years or so. What scientists don't know, and what they want to find out, is why this peak happens every eleven years.

Using telescopes and **satellites**, scientists are working to solve the mysteries of our spotty sun.

Satellite

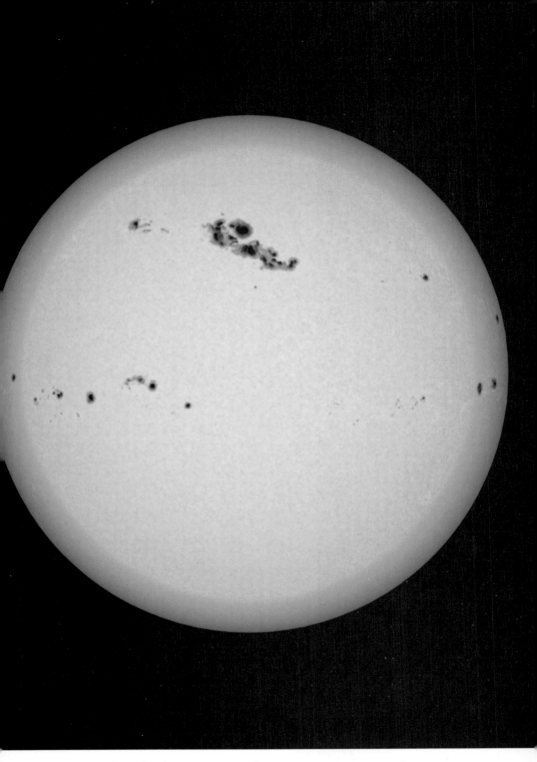

The dark spots on the sun are magnetic
storms called sunspots.

Pluto

Neptune

Uranus

Saturn

Jupiter

Mars

Earth

Venus

Mercury

Sun

Our sun is actually a star. It's the only star in our solar system. The sun seems much bigger than other stars because it's so close to us. You might not think the sun is close to us, because it is 93 million miles (150 million kilometers) away. For a star, though, that is very close.

The sun is a gigantic ball of incredibly hot, fiery gases. Inside the sun, its gases squeeze together. This squeezing heats the gases and sets off a huge chain of explosions deep inside the sun. We call these explosions **nuclear fusion**.

The energy from the sun's nuclear explosions

Our solar system

pours out into space as heat and light. Only a small part of the sun's heat and light reach Earth. Plants need the sun's light to grow. Animals need its warmth. Life on Earth could not exist without the sun's energy.

Like Earth, the sun is magnetic. Scientists describe this by saying the sun has a **magnetic field**. Within its magnetic field, the sun has north and south magnetic poles, just as Earth does.

One pole, or end, of the sun has a positive magnetic charge. The other pole of the sun has a negative charge. The positive and negative magnetic charges work to create the force of the magnetic field. The sun has **magnetic field lines** that can swoop out of its north magnetic pole, loop into space, and return to its south magnetic pole.

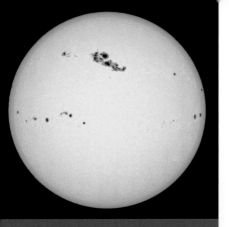

Low solar activity

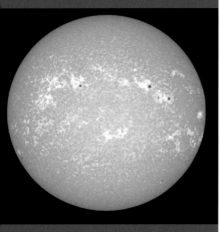

Moderate solar activity

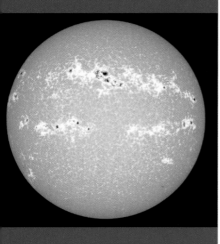

High solar activity

Why do stormy sunspots break out on the sun's surface? And why do the number of sunspots build up to a peak every eleven years or so? Scientists now know that the eleven-year sunspot cycle is connected to the sun's magnetic poles and its magnetic field lines.

The beginning of the sunspot cycle is called **solar minimum**. At that time, there is not much sunspot activity. Also, at that time, the sun's magnetic field is strongest at its north and south magnetic poles.

Over the next eleven years, the sun's magnetic field begins to get stronger near its middle, or equator. Its field lines also start to get twisted and tangled together, like a twisted garden hose. When the field lines twist and tangle, scientists think the tangled areas bunch together more and more. These tangled, bunched magnetic areas build up, resulting in sunspots and other storms. These storms on the sun build up to the peak of **solar maximum**, or solar max, about five years after solar minimum.

When solar max is reached, something very strange happens on the sun. Let's suppose that the sun's magnetic north pole and its geographic north pole were in the same place at the start of the sunspot cycle.

After five years or so, at solar max, the magnetic poles switch places! The positive

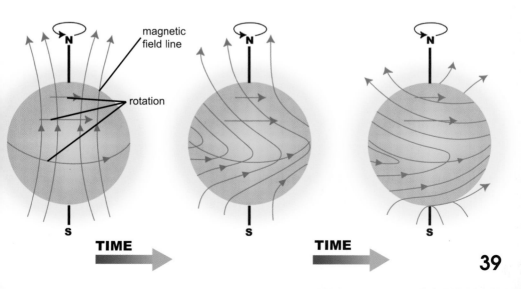

TIME

TIME

This satellite orbits the sun, gathering information on the sun's cycle.

magnetic charge at the north pole weakens and then becomes negative.

At the same time, the negative magnetic charge at the south pole weakens and then becomes positive. The sun's magnetic poles actually reverse their positions!

Over the next six or so years, the sunspot cycle begins to quiet down. At the end of this quieting down, solar minimum is reached. When that happens, the sun's magnetic poles are strong again but in the opposite positions of where they were at the previous solar minimum.

No one fully understands yet why the sun reverses its magnetic poles so often, or all the reasons for its sunspot cycle. However, scientists are learning more each year about the sunspot cycle and how it is linked to sun storms. Satellites are helping scientists gather this new information.

Why do scientists care about the sun's energy cycle? Storms on the sun can cause big problems here on Earth. So scientists watch for sunspots and even bigger storms on the sun to warn us.

Sometimes a sunspot explodes in a violent storm called a **solar flare**. Solar flares send intense blasts of energy shooting out from the sun in waves of heat, light, and

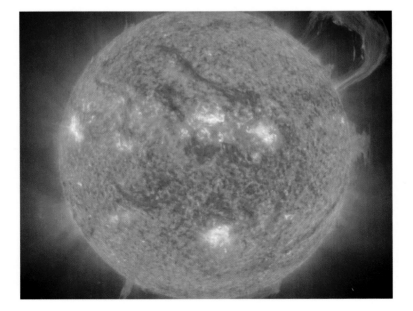

The light areas on the sun are where solar flares are taking place.

radiation. In fact, a solar flare may release as much energy as ten million hydrogen bombs. When some of that energy hits Earth, it can black out radio transmissions. It can also disrupt the signals used to guide ships and planes.

The biggest and most dangerous solar storms are called **coronal mass ejections**, or **CMEs**. When CMEs reach Earth, they can overload our electrical grids and cause huge power blackouts. They can also disable the satellites we use for phone and other communications.

The sun's storms can cause big problems for us on Earth, but the sun still does much more good than harm. Without the sun, Earth would be a bitterly cold, dead planet.

GLOSSARY

asteroid a large chunk of rock that floats in space

atmosphere the layer of air around Earth

carbon dioxide a gas made up of oxygen and carbon

comet a chunk of ice and rock that travels around the sun

coronal mass ejection (CME) a huge, stormy eruption of a cloud of energy from the sun into space

Hubble Space Telescope a device that has sent back many images of Uranus and other planets

hydrogen bomb a bomb that uses nuclear fusion to release energy, resulting in a massive explosion

magnetic field the area around a planet or the sun that is affected by its magnetic force

magnetic field lines lines that represent the magnetic force of a planet, the sun, or other object

meteorite a rock from outer space that reaches Earth's surface

methane a gas made up of hydrogen and carbon

nuclear fusion a process of combining atoms that releases energy inside the sun or in a hydrogen bomb

orbit the path that one space object takes when it travels around another

poles the northern and southern magnetic ends of stars, planets, and moons

remote located far away

satellite an object that orbits another object

solar flare a violent storm on the sun that sends blasts of energy shooting out in waves of heat, light, and radiation

solar maximum the highest point of the sunspot cycle

solar minimum the lowest point of the sunspot cycle

solar system the sun and all the planets and other objects that move around it

sunspot a magnetic storm on the sun that looks dark compared to the area around it

theory an idea that has not been proven

volcano a mountain with an opening through which fire, gas, and melted rock pour out

FIND OUT MORE

A Mysterious Fireball
http://www.psi.edu/projects/siberia/siberia.html
This site recreates the 1908 explosion in Siberia using eyewitness accounts.

The Mystery of the Spiral Canyons
www.space.com/scienceastronomy/mars_spirals_040325.html
Read more about Jon Pelletier's explanation of why strange spirals form in Mars' ice caps.

Life on Mars?
http://www.pbs.org/wgbh/nova/mars/
Go behind the scenes of a NOVA documentary and find out what scientists are learning about the Red Planet and whether life can exist there.

The Sun's Mysterious Spots
http://www.astro.uva.nl/demo/od95/
Take a virtual tour of the sun and learn more about our closest star.

More Books to Read

Don't Know Much about the Solar System by Kenneth C. Davis, HarperTrophy, 2001

Life on Mars by David Getz, Henry Holt & Company, 2004

Sun by Robin Kerrod, Lerner Publishing, 2003

INDEX

PHOTO CREDITS

MEET THE AUTHOR

Rosanna Hansen has worked in children's publishing as an author, editor-in-chief, and publishing executive. Most recently, she served as publisher and editor-in-chief of *Weekly Reader*, supervising seventeen classroom magazines as well as books. Previously, she was group publisher of Reader's Digest Children's Books.

Hansen has written more than fifteen children's books, including several on astronomy and space exploration. Her books on space include *My First Book of Space*; *Seeing Stars: The Milky Way and Its Constellations*; and another True Tales book, titled *Space*. In addition, she has written two other books in the True Tales series: *Caring Animals* and *Animal Rescuers*.

In her free time, she enjoys stargazing, visiting planetariums and observatories, and volunteering for Guiding Eyes for the Blind and for the Cheetah Conservation Fund in Africa. She and her husband, Corwith, live in Tuckahoe, New York.